Energy in Action

Suzanne Barchers

Consultant

Michelle Alfonsi
Engineer, Southern California
Aerospace Industry

Image Credits: Cover & p.1 iStock, pp.5–6 Blend
Images/Alamy; pp.18–19 caia image/Alamy; p.24
mauritius images GmbH/Alamy; pp.26–27 YAY
Media AS/Alamy; pp.6–9, 20 (illustrations) Tim
Bradley; pp. 13 (top middle),15, 16–17 (top), 22 (left),
23 Lexa Hoang; p.14 Deanne Fitzmaurice; pp.2–3,
6–7, 9 (background), 10, 12–13 (background),
20–21 (background), 22, 25, 30–31 iStock; pp.28–29
(illustration) Janelle Bell-Martin; p.13 (top right,
bottom right) SPL/Science Source; p.11 (left)
Andrew Syred/Science Source; p.11 (right) Steve
Gschmeissner/Science Source; all other images
from Shutterstock.

Library of Congress Cataloging-in-Publication Data

Barchers, Suzanne I., author.
  Energy in action / Suzanne Barchers.
    pages cm
  Summary: "Going to school and learning takes energy.
Playing a sport or an instrument requires energy, too.
Talking with friends, brushing your teeth, putting on
your pajamas, all take energy! But what is energy?
And how do we use it?"— Provided by publisher.
  Audience: K to grade 3.
  Includes index.
  ISBN 978-1-4807-4643-5 (pbk.)
  ISBN 978-1-4807-5087-6 (ebook)
1. Energy metabolism—Juvenile literature. I. Title.
  QP176.B363 2015
  531.6—dc23
                                        2014034266

Teacher Created Materials

5301 Oceanus Drive
Huntington Beach, CA 92649-1030
http://www.tcmpub.com

ISBN 978-1-4807-4643-5

Table of Contents

Feel the Power!

Brrrring! How do you feel when it's time to wake up? Do you spring out of bed? Are you charged up and ready to start your day? If so, you're full of energy. At least, that's one way to think of energy. It's the way many people think about it.

But scientists must be very precise with their words. They only use the word *energy* to describe the ability to move or change something. This kind of energy isn't something you can see or hold in your hands. But you can see what it does. You can tell that energy is working by what it does. And it does a lot!

Energy comes in many forms. Food has energy. The sun, plants, batteries, and many more things have energy. But whatever form it's in, energy is what makes things happen!

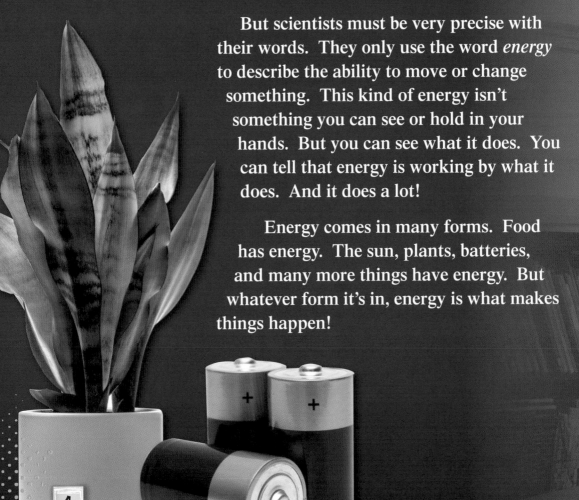

Energy can't be created or destroyed. It's pretty mind blowing when you think about it! That means the universe has the same amount of energy it had 13.8 billion years ago when it began!

Energy comes in two forms: potential energy and kinetic energy. And it's constantly changing back and forth between these forms. You may study the energy of a star or the energy of a bowl of soup. Either way, you need to ask two questions about the object you're studying. Where is it? And is it moving?

A moving ball hits a still ball.

Energy inside stars prevents them from collapsing on themselves.

The yellow ball transfers its energy to the red ball.

The yellow ball is now still, and the red ball is in motion.

Potential energy is related to the **position** of an object. Think about how tight a rubber band feels when it's pulled. You know that if you let it go, it will snap! It has the potential to be active. But until you let it go, the energy it has is stored. This stored energy is called *potential energy*.

Turning Potential into Kinetic

Both potential and kinetic energy are found in swinging objects. At the top of an object's path, it has potential energy. As it swings up and down, it has kinetic energy. When it reaches the top again, its kinetic energy turns back into potential energy. Whee!

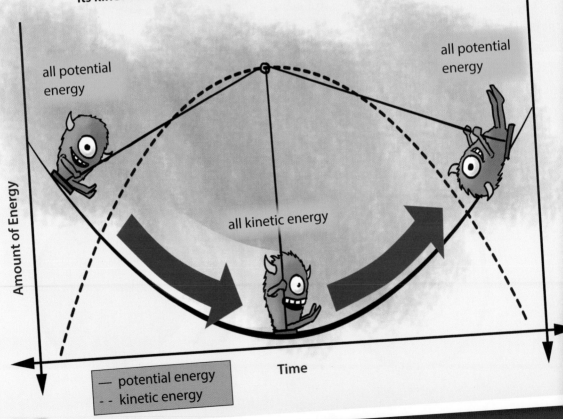

all potential energy

all potential energy

all kinetic energy

Amount of Energy

Time

— potential energy
- - kinetic energy

Up high, this rock has a lot of potential energy to squish any monsters in its way.

Look Out Below!

Objects high above the ground have more potential energy than objects that are close to the ground.

Down on the ground, the rock will no longer have any potential energy.

Kinetic energy is found wherever there is motion. When that rubber band is released, potential energy is transformed into kinetic energy. Whoosh! The rubber band goes flying! Cars, bicycles, and windmills all have kinetic energy when they move.

Storing Energy

You can't stretch a rubber band forever. Your arms would get too tired! And we can't use rubber bands to power our lives. We need to be able to convert potential energy, like that found in a stretched rubber band, into kinetic energy. Then, we can store it and use it whenever we need it. To do that, we need to know what's creating all this kinetic energy.

Everything in the world is made of matter. And all matter is made up of **atoms**. **Protons** are found at the center of atoms. They have a positive charge. The center of the atom is called the *nucleus*. **Electrons** surround the nucleus. They have a negative charge. Protons and electrons are opposites. And opposites attract. As a result, the protons keep the electrons from flying away.

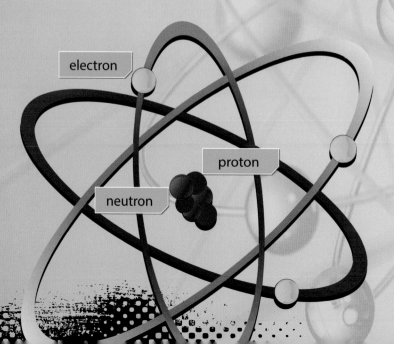

electron

proton

neutron

Macro and Micro

Atoms, molecules, and bacteria are microscopic. Microscopic objects are things that are too small to see with our eyes. Macroscopic objects are things we can see with our eyes. Both macroscopic and microscopic objects can have kinetic energy.

Eyelash mites are microscopic organisms that live on hair follicles.

In most cases, the nucleus also has **neutrons**. They aren't positive or negative. They are neutral. In other words, they are balanced and have no charge. They are found with the protons at the center of the atom.

Atoms combine to create **molecules**. Molecules slide, float, bounce, and combine to make up everything around us. And that means everything has energy. It's the energy of moving atoms and molecules. And they're always spinning, vibrating, stretching, and bending.

Chemical Energy

Just like stretched rubber bands have stored energy, molecules have stored energy in the **bonds** between their atoms. This is chemical energy. When those bonds are broken, energy is released. And new molecules with new bonds may form.

Chemical energy is used for many things. Food provides people with chemical energy. When we eat, our bodies use the chemical energy that is stored in food. Batteries use chemical energy to create electricity. Plants use sunlight to break the bonds of carbon dioxide and water to create energy. Every chemical has the ability to release energy.

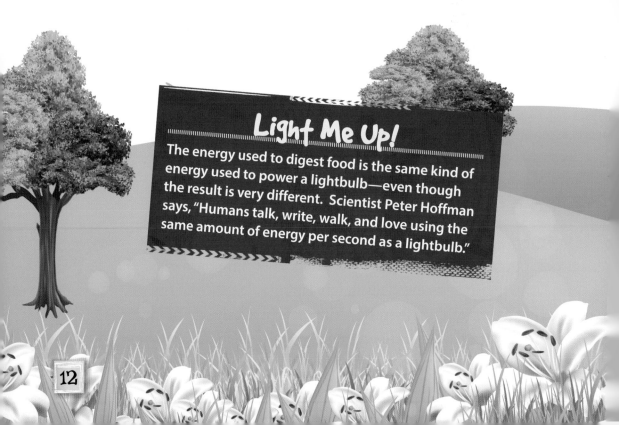

Light Me Up!

The energy used to digest food is the same kind of energy used to power a lightbulb—even though the result is very different. Scientist Peter Hoffman says, "Humans talk, write, walk, and love using the same amount of energy per second as a lightbulb."

carbon dioxide

water

sugar

Photosynthesis

During photosynthesis, plants absorb carbon dioxide from the air and water from the ground. Sunlight breaks the bonds in the molecules. The atoms rearrange to create sugar. The plant uses this for energy.

Nuclear Energy

Nuclear energy is another form of stored energy. It's stored tightly in the nucleus of an atom. There are two ways to release this energy. One way is through fusion. Fusion combines atoms to make new atoms. The sun uses fusion to make light and thermal, or heat, energy. The other way is through fission. Fission splits atoms into smaller atoms. Every time an atom splits, it gives off energy. That triggers a chain reaction. When the smaller atoms are created, less energy is required to hold them together. So heat and light are released. Nuclear reactors at power plants produce electricity using fission.

Mental Energy

Taylor Wilson was 12 years old when he decided to make a star in a jar. By the time he was 14, he had built a nuclear fusion reactor in his parents' garage! He used the reactor to study the fusion that takes place inside the sun.

CAUTION
RAW URANIUM ORE

RADIATION AREA

Fusion

Inside the sun, hydrogen atoms combine to form helium.

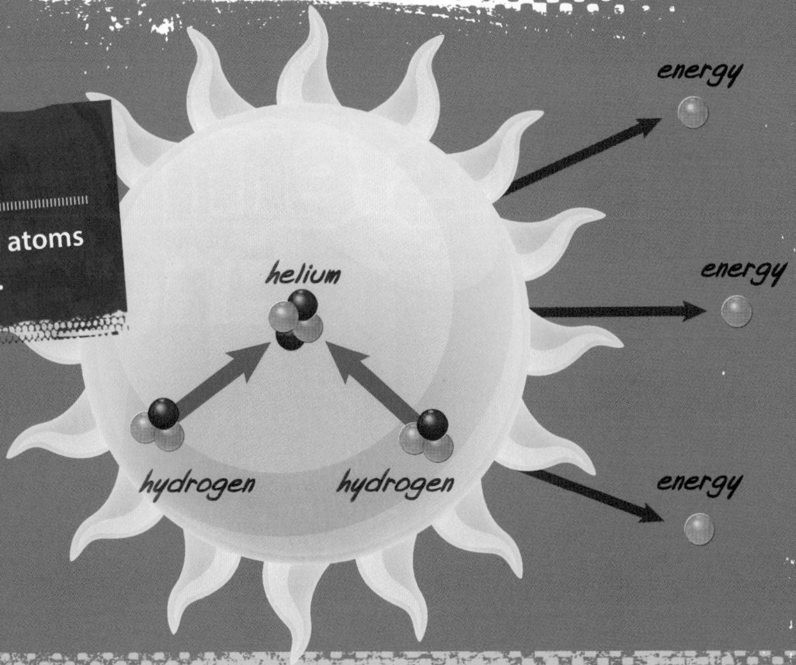

energy

energy

energy

helium

hydrogen   hydrogen

energy

Fission

Fission is similar to the beginning of a game of pool. One neutron is used to break up the large atom into smaller atoms.

atom

neutron

Transferring Energy

Energy is often transferred between objects. Think about two objects colliding, or crashing into each other. For example, when one ball hits another ball, the energy is transferred from one to the other. But it's not as if one ball just hands the other all of its energy. So how does this work?

Heat Wave

Energy can be transferred in the form of heat in three ways: convection, radiation, and conduction.

Convection transfers energy within a liquid or a gas.

Heat

Energy can be transferred in two ways. Heat is one way. We all know what heat feels like. When something is heated, its atoms move faster. They jump and wiggle in crazy ways.

Energy is transferred between objects when one is hotter than the other. Heat flows from hot areas to colder areas. Temperature is used to measure this kinetic energy. A high temperature means there's a lot of kinetic energy. A low temperature means there is less kinetic energy. Cool, right?

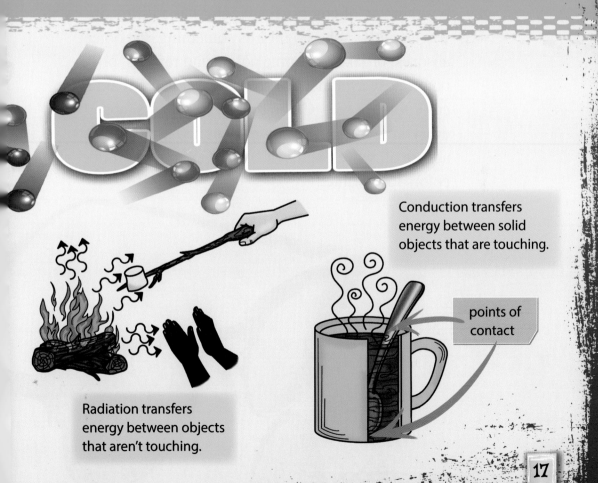

Conduction transfers energy between solid objects that are touching.

points of contact

Radiation transfers energy between objects that aren't touching.

Light

Better grab your sunglasses! Light is another way energy is transferred. It's a form of radiant energy, which is heat. We see it when we turn on lamps and when we go outside. The sun is the ultimate source of light for our planet. Plants rely on sunlight to grow. But there's more to light than what we can see.

A lightbulb gives off waves of light. The light may appear white, but inside that beam of light, there is a rainbow of colors. Each color has a different **wavelength**. When light hits something, the object absorbs, or takes in, some colors and reflects, or bounces away, others. The color that is reflected is the color that we see. Green things, like leaves, absorb everything except green wavelengths. Black objects absorb all wavelengths of light. Objects that reflect all colors look white.

A Spectrum of Waves

The electromagnetic spectrum is the full range of electromagnetic waves. It includes radio waves, which have low frequencies and long wavelengths, and gamma rays, which have high frequencies and short wavelengths.

Light travels faster than anything else in the universe!

gamma rays

x-rays

ultraviolet

visible light

infrared

microwaves

radio waves

19

Work

Energy can also be transferred in the form of **work**. Just like *heat*, the word *work* has a different meaning in science. It doesn't mean "the thing your parents do to earn money." Instead, *work* refers to the motion of atoms, molecules, and larger objects. Work moves things from place to place.

Usually, people think of work being done in ways we can see. Pushing a hippo up a hill takes a whole lot of effort. Scientists call that work, just like everyone else. Work is done when a force acts to move an object.

Higher Math

Scientists have studied a great deal to find the connection between work and heat. They have proven that work can be turned into heat. But the math says that heat can't completely be turned into work.

What's the difference between heat and work? They both transfer energy, but the energy transfer in work is more orderly. It's as if the atoms are lined up like soldiers, marching from one place to another. To the contrary, heat results when atoms move randomly.

Electrical Energy

The modern world is filled with electrical energy. It's not something we can see, but it powers our video games, phones, and more. Electrical energy is the flow of electrons through the world. It can be used to transfer energy into light. Or it can be transferred into mechanical energy. Tools like power drills transfer electricity into mechanical energy. When electricity powers a power drill, the drill parts move. When the force of the spinning drill head is used to drill a hole, work is done.

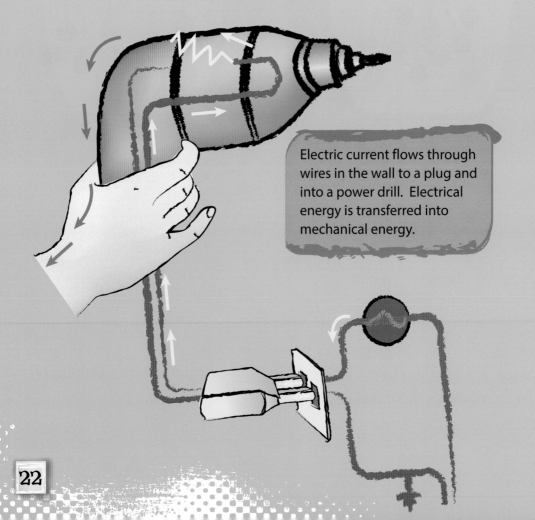

Electric current flows through wires in the wall to a plug and into a power drill. Electrical energy is transferred into mechanical energy.

Electricity is the energy produced by electrons in motion. A neutral atom has an equal number of protons and electrons. But atoms gain and lose electrons. This makes the atoms positive or negative. Atoms seek balance. When they have a positive charge, they attract electrons. When they are negative, they push them away. First, a negative atom sheds an electron. That lost electron jumps to the next atom. The new atom sheds an electron. The cycle continues on and on. The result is a flow of energy.

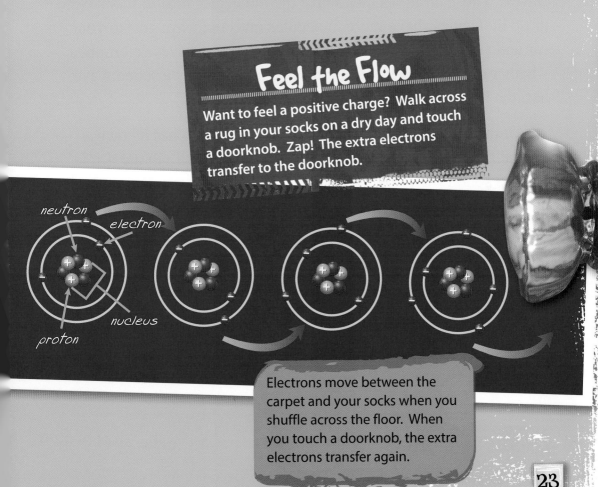

Feel the Flow

Want to feel a positive charge? Walk across a rug in your socks on a dry day and touch a doorknob. Zap! The extra electrons transfer to the doorknob.

neutron

electron

nucleus

proton

Electrons move between the carpet and your socks when you shuffle across the floor. When you touch a doorknob, the extra electrons transfer again.

Sound

Sounds keep us safe. They alert us of danger. They can also be very beautiful. Music and kind words warm our hearts. Everything from a low drum roll to a sharp bird chirp are sounds we hear. These sounds are forms of kinetic energy. Sound is the movement of **vibrations** through matter. Sound is another form of work.

Sound waves vibrate molecules. Try clapping your hands together. The impact of your hands causes air molecules to move in waves. Those air molecules shake the molecules next to them. And those molecules shake more molecules until the wave gets to your ear and you hear the clap. The frequency of the waves determines whether the sound is low or high. The more energy a sound wave has, the louder it sounds.

All matter vibrates in some way. So everything has its own natural frequency. This is the speed at which it will vibrate if it is hit by a sound wave. If a person sings at the same **pitch** as a glass's natural frequency, the sound will vibrate the air molecules around the glass. If the sound is loud enough, it can cause the glass to vibrate, as well. And if the glass vibrates too much, it will break!

Scientists have used powerful sound waves to make objects float!

24

Pitch

The pitch of a sound is how high or low the sound is. It is determined by the frequency, which is the number of times the wave repeats in a second.

Low-pitched sounds, such as a drum, have a low frequency.

High-pitched sounds, such as a bird chirping, have a high frequency.

The Flow of Energy

The amount of energy in the universe never changes. Energy can't be created or destroyed. But energy is constantly changing from one form to another. Potential energy turns into kinetic energy. Electrical energy can be turned into mechanical energy. Chemical energy can be turned into thermal energy. But really, it's all energy. It's what powers our world.

Think Like a Scientist

How much potential energy does a slingshot have? Experiment and find out!

What to Get

- 2 large rubber bands
- 2 small, thin rubber bands
- 2 large marshmallows
- 4 toilet paper tubes
- hole punch
- pencil
- scissors
- tape

What to Do

1. Cut one toilet paper tube in half. Roll it tightly and tape it back together. Punch two holes on opposite edges of the roll. Push the pencil through the holes.

2. Cut two short slits on the edge of the other toilet paper tube (about the width of your finger). Repeat this for the opposite side of the same end.

3. Attach a large rubber band to each set of slits. Tape the rubber bands in place.

4. Slide your first tube into the second one. Hook the rubber bands around each end of the pencil.

5. Repeat steps one to four to make a slingshot with the small rubber bands.

6. Load a marshmallow into the top of each slingshot. Shoot the marshmallows. How far does each go? Which slingshot has the most potential and kinetic energy? Why?

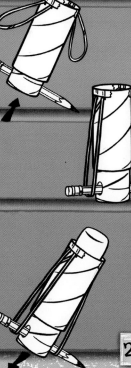

Glossary

atoms—tiny particles that make up all matter

bonds—forces that hold atoms together in molecules

electrons—particles that have negative charges and travel around the nucleus of atoms

molecules—the smallest possible amounts of a particular substance that have all the characteristics of the substance

neutrons—particles that have neutral charges and are part of the nucleus of atoms

pitch—the highness or lowness of a sound

position—the place where something is in relation to other things

protons—particles that have positive charges and are part of the nucleus of atoms

vibrations—rapid motions of particles back and forth

wavelength—the distance between two peaks of the same wave

work—the transfer of energy that results from a force moving an object

Index

Your Turn!

Energy Observations

Find a place to sit inside. Observe the types of energy that are in action around you. Record your observations. Then, find a safe place to sit outside. Observe the types of energy that are in action around you. Record your observations. Compare and contrast the energy you observed.